Colors of Christmas

A Joyful Celebration of the Season

D1413714

Colors of Christmas

A Joyful Celebration of the Season

Compiled by PHIL BARFOOT
Arranged and Orchestrated by LARI GOSS

Companion Materials

Choral Book	0 80689 35017 7
Cassette	0 80689 65534 0
Compact Disc	0 80689 65522 7
CD Trax (Split)	0 80689 69812 5
CD Trax (Stereo)	0 80689 69842 2
PracticeTrax	0 80689 59044 3
Studio Orchestration	0 80689 35767 1
Bulk CDs (10 pak)*	0 80689 60972 5

*This package of 10 Compact Discs provides an inexpensive way for
your choir members to have their own copy of the recording.*

Instrumentation

FLUTE 1, 2	Bb TENOR SAXOPHONE/BARITONE T.C.	VIOLIN 1, 2*
OBOE	(doubles Trombone 1, 2)	VIOLA*
Bb CLARINET	Bb TRUMPET 1, 2, 3	CELLO/BASSOON
BASS CLARINET	FRENCH HORN 1, 2, 3	ARCO BASS
(doubles Tuba)	TROMBONE 1, 2, 3	RHYTHM
Eb ALTO SAXOPHONE	TUBA	HARP
(doubles F Horn)	PERCUSSION 1, 2	STRING REDUCTION
	*simplified parts included	

Edited by *Rob Howard* and *Ken Barker*

Art Design by *Philpott Design*

Transcribed and Engraved by
Bill Wolaver and David Thibodeaux

Production Coordination by *Sundy Goodnight*

 This symbol indicates a track number on the Accompaniment Compact Disc. Selecting a given CD track
number will start the accompaniment track at the corresponding musical section indicated in the choral book.

Printed by Davis Brothers Printing, Waco, Texas

Foreword

The spectrum of colors, emotions, feelings and traditions that the Christmas season offers create an eclectic and unique palate upon which the Minister of Music can design his or her Christmas production.

After the extremely positive response to last year's *Portraits of Christmas*, we wanted to offer a sequel that had the energy, freshness, warmth, creativity and "special moments" that you need when creating a Christmas production or concert that will make a lasting impact in your church.

To accomplish this, we again drew on the imagination and creativity of various Ministers of Music across America who served on the creative team for *Colors of Christmas*.

The suggestions and ideas compiled from this team were absolutely incredible! A very special thanks to each of these outstanding Ministers of Music for their invaluable help in determining the content and style of this unique project.

The "colors" and "moments" that many of you requested have resulted in a unique and eclectic mix of styles which include high-energy celebration songs, warm nostalgic moments, fresh contemporary settings, seasonal favorites and meaningful worship moments that will help you in making this season a very special one in your church.

Also included is Amy Grant's Christmas classic, "A Christmas to Remember" and Avalon's very popular "Light a Candle," which lends itself to a wonderful candle lighting opportunity and use of children's choir. The staging possibilities with "The Little Drummer Boy" and "Celebrate the Season Medley" are great as well.

It is our desire that this collection will take you and your congregation on a journey that will be full of the excitement, celebration and joy of the season, yet, most importantly, lead to the worship and adoration of the Savior whose birthday we celebrate.

God's BEST to you as you prepare and present *Colors of Christmas*.

Blessings!
Phil Barfoot and Lari Goss

A special thanks to each of the following Ministers of Music and choirs who helped to create this project and participated in the original custom recordings:

Herb Armentrout,
Minister of Music
Broadmoor Baptist Church
Shreveport, LA
Dr. Chuck Pourciau, Pastor

Dr. Phil Barfoot,
Minister of Music
Thompson Station Baptist
Church
Thompson Station, TN
Dr. Thomas J. McCoy, Pastor

Norman Behymer,
Minister of Worship
Council Road Baptist Church
Bethany, OK
Dr. Mark Hartman, Pastor

Trent Blackley,
Minister of Music & Worship
First Baptist Church
Sunnyvale, TX
Dr. Charles L. Wilson, Pastor

James Bradford,
Minister of Worship
First Southern Baptist Church
Oklahoma City, OK
Dr. Thomas D. Elliff, Pastor

Ron Cochran,
Minister of Music
Portland Christian Center
Portland, OR
Bill Wilson, Pastor

Darrell Cummings,
Minister of Music
Big Valley Grace Community
Church
Modesto, CA

Miller Cunningham,
Pastor of Worship & Music
Germantown Baptist Church
Germantown, TN
Dr. Sam Shaw, Pastor

Mark Deakins, Chairman,
Department of Music
Kentucky Christian College
Grayson, KY

Carlton Dillard,
Associate Pastor of Worship
Riverbend Church
Austin, TX
Dr. Gerald Mann, Pastor

Keith Ferguson,
Minister of Music
First Baptist Church
Dallas, TX
Dr. Mac Brunson, Jr., Pastor

Joe Fitzpatrick,
Minister of Music
Park Hill Baptist Church
North Little Rock, AR
Dr. S. Cary Heard, Pastor

Rob Flint,
Associate Pastor of
Praise and Worship
McGregor Baptist Church
Ft Myers, FL
Dr. Richard Powell, Pastor

Art Fulks,
Associate Pastor of
Music and Worship
Jersey Baptist Church
Pataskala, OH
John A. Hays, Pastor

Manuel Garcia II,
Associate Pastor of Music
First Baptist Church
Panama City, FL
Craig Conner, Pastor

Rocky L. Gillmore,
Worship Pastor
Crossroads Baptist Church
The Woodlands, TX
Larry York, Pastor

O. D. Hall Jr.,
Minister of Music
Magnolia Avenue Baptist
Church
Riverside, CA
Dr. Montia Setzler, Pastor

Ken Hartley,
Pastor of Worship and Praise
First Baptist Church of
Indian Rocks
Largo, FL
Dr. Charlie Martin, Pastor

Charles Heinz,
Minister of Music
Central Church
Collierville, TN
Dr. Jimmy Latimer, Pastor

Dick Hill,
Pastor, Worship Ministries
Champion Forest Baptist
Church
Houston, TX
Dr. Damon Shook, Pastor

Ed Keyes,
Minister of Music
Cottage Hill Baptist Church
Mobile, AL
Dr. Allan Lockerman, Pastor

Robbin Kuder,
Associate Pastor of Worship
Northwoods Baptist Church
Tallahassee, FL
John Rickenbacker, Jr., Pastor

Michael McGrew,
Minister of Music & Worship
Palma Sola Bay Baptist Church
Bradenton, FL

Simeon Nix,
Associate Pastor,
Music Ministries
Bell Shoals Baptist Church
Brandon, FL
Dr. Ken Alford, Pastor

C. Warren Pearson,
Minister of Worship & Music
Southcliff Baptist Church
Fort Worth, TX
Dr. Carroll Marr, Pastor

Gregory M. Stahl,
Associate Pastor,
Music & Worship
Williams Trace Baptist Church
Sugarland, TX
Dr. Phil Lineberger, Pastor

Greg Toney,
Minister of Music
Calvary Baptist Church
Clearwater, FL
Dr. Bill Anderson, Pastor

Pat Van Dyke,
Associate Pastor of Worship
First Baptist Church
Clarkesville, TN
Dr. Roger Freeman, Pastor

If your church would be interested in utilizing these arrangements and tracks for a custom recording, contact Phil Barfoot at Christian Copyright Alliance, 9484 Foothills Drive, Brentwood, TN 37027, (615) 599-8326, ccapb@aol.com.

Contents

in alphabetical order

Gloria

with

Glory, Glory

Words and Music by
MARK HAYES
Arranged by Lari Goss

Glo - ry be un - to God on high.

Glo - ri - a in ex - cel - sis De - o; Peace on earth, good

(Back to pg. 11)

will to ev - 'ry - one.

(Back to pg. 11)

14

17

breaking through the night.

Glo - ri - a in ex - cel - sis De - o;

Glo - ry be un - to God on high.

85

Glo-ri-a in__ ex-cel-sis__ De - o; Peace on earth,__ good

F(no3) F/A C G/B Gsus/A G D/F♯ G

88

will to ev-'ry-one._____ Glo-ri-a!

E/G♯ Am G/B C C/D G

91 **6** With energy! ♩ = 162

N.C. G G♯/F♯ A/F B♭/E B/D♯ C/D

f

GLORY, GLORY! (Amerson/Clydesdale)

22

26

Joy to the World! Hallelujah!

Arranged by Lari Goss

32

HALLELUJAH CHORUS (Handel)

34

36

38

42

Celebrate the Season Medley

includes

Winter Wonderland, Let It Snow, I'll Be Home for Christmas,
and **It's the Most Wonderful Time of the Year**

Arranged by Lari Goss

WINTER WONDERLAND (Bernard/Smith)

46

50

I'LL BE HOME FOR CHRISTMAS (Gannon/Kent)

58

23 *IT'S THE MOST WONDERFUL TIME OF THE YEAR (Pola/Wyle)*

61

Agnus Dei

with
O Come, Let Us Adore Him

**Words and Music by
MICHAEL W. SMITH**
Arranged by Lari Goss

68

70

72

O COME, LET US ADORE HIM (Traditional/Wade's Cantus Diversi, 1751)

74

The Little Drummer Boy

Words and Music by
KATHERINE DAVIS, HENRY ONORITI
and HARRY SIMEONE
Arranged by Lari Goss

Close to the consonant "m" early, throughout the song—let the tone continue to vibrate.

This Little Child

Words and Music by
SCOTT WESLEY BROWN
Arranged by Lari Goss

2. Man-y years___ have come and gone,_ yet this world re-mains the same.

1. Who would have thought that long a-go,___ so ver-y far a-way, a

86

92

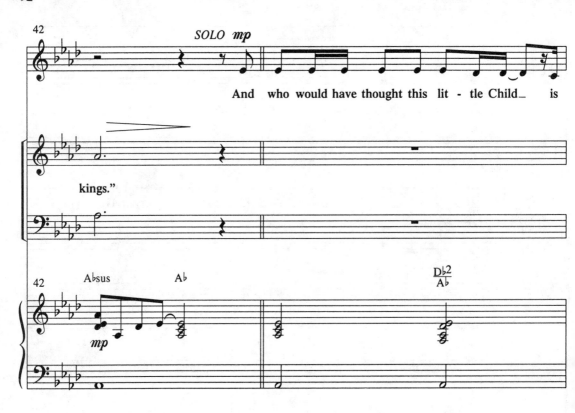

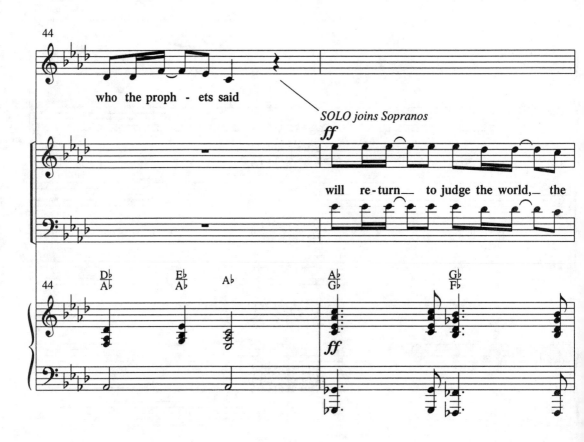

94

Light a Candle

with
Silent Night! Holy Night!

Words and Music by
JOEL LINDSAY and WAYNE HAUN
Arranged by Lari Goss

for the wo-man who is lone - ly__ and ev-'ry

Christ - mas it's the same. For the chil-dren who need__ more than pres -

- ents can bring,__

CHOIR *mp*

Light a can - dle,__

47

D.S. al CODA 𝄋
(Back to pg. 98)

(Back to pg. 98)

o - pen our hearts__ to shine through__ the__ dark?

Ebm   Db   Cb2

D.S. al CODA 𝄋
(Back to pg. 98)

CODA

(SOLO)

mf

And   in this spe - cial time__ of year,__ may

CODA

Ebmaj7   Gb6

34

peace on earth— sur - round— us here— and teach us there's— a bet - ter way— to live..

Db2/F   Db/F   Dbm/Fb

36

—— And with ev - 'ry flame— that burns,—

Ab/Eb   Dbmaj7   Cm7   Fm7

we must some - how learn___

that love's the great - est gift that

we could ev - er give.___

106

108

CHILDREN'S CHOIR (opt. WOMEN)

Sleep⸺ in heav - en - ly peace.

Una Fiesta Navidad
(Angels We Have Heard on High)

Traditional French carol
Arranged by Lari Goss

112

114

116

123

A Christmas to Remember

Words and Music by
AMY GRANT, BEVERLY DARNALL
and CHRIS EATON
Arranged by Lari Goss

may - be   they   will___ come   true.___

O Happy Day

Words and Music by
EDWIN HAWKINS
Arranged by Lari Goss

144

(SOLO cont. ad lib.)

was born on Christ - mas day!_____

(Back to pg. 149)